A War Between the Eyes

Battling Mental Illness

By Evan Wallace
Illustration By Svetlana Wunnenberg

Copyright Information

Acknowledgements

I would consider myself hard to handle. But, in the days leading up to the drafting of this book, I came to my breaking point. For so long, recognizing the fact that help was sometimes necessary seemed foreign. Looking in the mirror, all I could see was disappointment, someone broken, someone unworthy of help. Yet, at my rock bottom, my moment of unforgiving sadness, those I was close to did not turn a blind eye. So they deserve the credit, for they saved my life and gave me the chance to find this new purpose.

Thank you,
Mom- for being my best friend through it all, helping me to become my best self and to learn to ask for help
Grandma and Grandpa- for always making sure I was taken care of, from when I was a baby until now, I knew I could always count on you to be there
Erin and Matt- for giving me your guidance and showing me how to deal with the change of life. I can't forget to mention the many good meals you both paid for.
John- for pulling me off the side of the road and for talking through my worry all these years

Chapter One

On the Front Lines

A War Between the Eyes

A war between the eyes
Greatest fight of all one might surmise
Where the enemy is always a step ahead
And you struggle to even rest your head
Each day brings tears to your eyes
As you trek through a valley formed by lies
Off to the next battle the leader rages
Lacking the luck of fools and sages
He watches as his plan slowly dies
Another lost to the war between the eyes

My Runaway Bride

My runaway bride
Millions of emotions yearned inside
I was left there standing at the altar
Knowing I was the one to falter
My mistakes amplified more and more with each step
Realizing that she was the one that wept

My runaway bride
Her eyes making our emotions collide
The heavenly bells she had waited for
Those same bells meant nothing anymore
My actions were so vain
At least when I was sober I couldn't cause her pain

I found out a week later what the stress had done
Gone with the bang of a loaded gun, the pain had finally
won
I now live a life full of regret
Like looking in the mirror at someone you've just met
Fifty years later and I lay here ready to go
To the place only the passed know
Although she lived a shorter life than me
I wonder why it just couldn't be
I guess you could say that the day that I died
Was the day I lost my runaway bride

Loss

Everyone experiences loss
So, why did it make me feel so cross
As it was no one's fault but mine
The heartache seemed to be a heavenly sign
For my soul was now in the ring
Where days there pain would bring
Pushing me down to my knees
From a pedestal of pride came the freeze
That would harden my heart to the beauty of the world
To nothing more than the abyss into which it was hurled

The Window

The internet is a window
Opening eyes to what lies beyond the pillow
Yet with this power we go blind
To the travesties that ravage the mind

How?

The keyboard is dangerous
Enter it says....
An entrance into a dark world
One for those that struggle
For the answers in which they have longed
How to get better?
Or more often, *How to end*?
There the ideas take form
Where the freefall from the airplane begins
Parachute cut..... Reaching *terminal* velocity

Cancer

A ravenous cancer fills our lives
Every passing moment it grows
Bringing us closer to our demise
Or closer to true salvation

Your life comes to one point
The culmination of love and tears
Death now stares you in the face
Trying to break you, to make you afraid
But what's next scares even death
As you tell death you are not afraid
Cause the only thing scarier than death itself...
Is not fearing it at all

Status Quo

Sometimes I can't wait to die
Then I wouldn't have to live this lie
A lie to myself that I am truly living
For I am but a cog in the wheel
Meant only to further the machine
One called the status quo
Who lives not by what is just or right
But who lives only for the calmness of night

Keep Asking

"What's Wrong?'
They all repeat their question
Frowns signal the worry
Yet I have no answer to give
Or I would solve it myself
But I was born with a problem
One in which the answer changes
As often as the question is asked

Wrong Emotions

Wrong emotions
Built by fantastical notions
Not cured by the strongest of potions
But running deeper than the oceans

Void

I feel pathetic
Helpless as a baby
Spineless as a worm
No sense of control
No feelings of comfort
I am but a symptom of the disease
One without a cure
One void of compassion

Glances

Everyone looked the same
Not in their appearance
But in their glances
The glances blinded them
From the weed smoking the air
From the violence dancing through the streets
From the rejection poking at their hearts
From the idea that I am not so different from them

Therapy 1

An exaggeration
Was that all it was?
All the fear was made up
The pain seemed meaningless
Every tear was forced
And time in therapy was wasted
Cause if I couldn't be believed by you
There was no path to better

Out of Control

Behind the wheel was control
The speed like a scream from the soul
Two lanes, no shoulder
Risk making every turn bolder
Until finally it all clicked
Where the grass was dew slicked
Turn the wheel to end it all
The car sliding as time seemed to stall

Three Weeks

Three weeks to kick in
With emotions so thin
And demons crawling within
Smirking their evil grin
Begging me to let them win
Making my head spin
As I fall like a pin
Until finally my body gives in

Recurrent Thoughts

Go away
Even for a day
Cause I need a break
From this thought of my wake
For everything I do
Brings me closer to you
And everything I say
Pushes me farther away

Gas Light

Wandering aimlessly
I drift into the other lane
Swerving to avoid the panic
Speeding away from the pressure
But everything has its limits
And the gas light is finally on
The car is slowing
My run has come to an end

Fragile

In the park, the plants flourished
Flowers of every color and every type
Swaying in the breeze of early spring
People stop to admire them
As they glisten in their full bloom
But winter has one last laugh
As a frost chills the air
And little by little the petals fall
Remnants of the fragile flowers
That before were so beautiful
Now lay broken, floating in the wind

Common Denominator

There's no excuse
And if there was then what's the use
Cause all I love is broken up
I'm worn and bruised

And there's no escape
From what I felt that day
You left me and now all I see
Is my mistakes

For I'm the thread
Like people have said
I'm the one, the only one
To cause this pain
To ruin everything

The common denominator
Standing in the rain

Evacuate

Sirens are blaring
Yet everyone is still
Evacuation warning in place
But outside offers no refuge
There lies the cold winter air
Further chilling the barren soul
For the fire offers comfort
The fire is salvation

Smoke Screen

Eyes are watering
The haze is thick
And nobody can find him

But we are so close now
Air seems to be fading fast
"We have to turn back" they scream
Walls are crumbling like sheets of paper

His memories burn, while their sympathy he spurns
For everything went according to plan
They'll never see this sad state of a man

Perfection

Failure like a ghost haunts me
A reminder of what I'll never be
Not someone's heartbeat
Not their song on repeat
Not one of the elite
But instead a *"delete"*
Cause this perfection isn't real
If it was, could it make me feel?

Panic Attack

My feet become heavy
As my head becomes light
The fear I feel is real
And its shame is hard to conceal
Nobody else is scared
But then again, no one else cared

It's just a test right?
No, it's a mental fright
If I close my eyes it will go away
The world turns a shade of gray
And my eyes begin to go heavy
Until I wake up to the light

Thief

You've taken my sanity
And now my hope
What more could you want from me?
I'm up against the ropes

You're a thief in the night
My devil in the day
Now what more can I say?
For my words lack power
More proof that I'm not okay

Cameras

Behind the camera lens
There are those that judge my sins
Making me feel like I'm crazy
Or maybe stupid, hopeless, or lazy
But they don't see the pain inside
The kind that lasts after the tears have dried
Instead they look down on me
Another name on the list of three
Living nothing but a sad exlstence
When all I need is to end the distance

Silence

There is victory in silence
As you've escaped worldly violence
Entering into the vastness of the mind
Yet even there, no one is kind
For thoughts are our biggest enemies
Singing out the heart's off tune melodies

Chapter Two
P.O.W.

White Walls
Injured in battle, I stare at White Walls
Reminders of my skin that crawls
Drifting through the sands of time
We sit begging for only one more dime
To become the person we wish we were
But instead forever, the white walls stir

Prisoner

Fifteen minutes
Then another room check
That's all I'm to be trusted
A threat to others and myself
No different than a prisoner on death row
But I wait for a verdict in my appeal
For that decides my fate
Whether I'm to be a prisoner in here
Or within my own skin

Voluntary

Someone help me
I can't escape these thoughts
I can't escape myself

Surrounded by guards
Watching my every move
Recording my every thought

I asked for this
This place in which most would go crazy
This place where I feel most sane

Cold Sheets

Laying between these cold sheets
The thin fabric draped onto the floor
Scorned by the comfort it was to promote
Taking a new form as we tossed and turned
Signaling our fluxing emotions
Signaling that change is hope

Therapy 2

"What are you?"
Never had it crossed my mind
I just was... Nothing more
Again they asked...
Labels. Experiences. Thoughts.
But that is not enough
What is my definition?
Definitions are standard
"So what are you?"
I am **Undefined**

Visiting Hours

Sickness brings with it a scar
But in this little time normal is not far
For on the other side of the table
Happiness like that of a fable
A reminder of what life is like
When you take control of the mic

Not Alone

They are trapped too
Fighting a battle which seems unwinnable
From all walks of life they have come
To be healed, to find solace in the darkness
They are so different from me
Yet they understand me better than anyone
Their pain is mine
Their fear is mine
But sitting alongside them, their strength is mine

Chapter Three
Coming Home

Can I heal?
The doctor's orders were clear
"Use these crutches as support"
Instead, I use them as a shield
Yet what do they protect me from?
From the pain that brings me to my knees
From the memories that haunt my dreams
No... they protect me from nothing
As I feel the rejection, I see their stares
They whisper as if I can't hear them
But the voices inside scream too
That I am weak, that I need validation
Without them can my wounds heal?

Normal

Reality rests in our eyes
Shaping how we see the skies
Fluffy clouds with animal shapes
Or dark monsters from which rain escapes
Drops fall caressing your cheek
Showing the monster you seek
That will soon be an animal again
"Normal" in the eyes of men

Checkmate

There aren't many pieces left
Both of us are fighting for control
Plotting against the other
Trying to think ten moves ahead
But as your pawn slides another
You begin to tremble
Regretting your choice to challenge me
Because I was always ahead
I just didn't know it until "Checkmate"

A State of Being

The lines are rules
The rumble strips are warnings
Driving on each now has new meaning
On how close I really was to not being
They are a reminder of new strength
And the help within arms reach

Lub Dub

For the first time I hear it
What had been hidden until now
The beat as strong as diamonds
The rhythm constant like spring rains
The warmth radiating as if from the sun
My heart's true song
Risen from the depths of the muck
Now plays loudly for all to hear
Claiming victory over fear

Friends

It burns brightest when it's fed
Shining in your eyes, the shades of deep red
Bringing those you care for together
To keep through the roughest weather
Making you realize what you truly desire
Those close friends keeping up your fire

Time (Take my hand)

It moves fastest when you want it to slow
Moving slowest when you've lost your glow
It's a measure of days gone past
It's a feeling you long for back
It's a reminder of all the love
So we look to the stars above
Hoping one day to understand
How to walk hand in hand

Renaissance of the Sky

Darkness falls across the land
With no question from beast or man
Idly sits the earth below
Watching the stars, night's heavenly glow
Everyone has a story to tell
Even those stars for which our hearts seem to yell

"The moon she glows like pearls in the gentle sea
And as I look above, the stars gaze down at me
Seeing all the love I've spent on her, I show not a bit of resent
Knowing not if she would love me too
For she does not speak, but I am in love with the sound I do not hear"

"The Sun" she silently thought, he is sombering again
"Why does he never speak to me?"
She quietly wept for he could not see
 "I love him she said, why does he do this to me?"
"Until tomorrow love, I have seen enough today"

Dreams
Eyes flutter as sun shines through the blinds
You almost got to see the ending this time
The light is a reminder of your truth
That life is not as fair as dreams

For years the pillow brings more of the same
Until finally your heart delivers the ending
The morning seems a little warmer
A feeling of calm like that of a sleeping baby
And like for them, the possibilities seem endless

Every fleeting moment
Every joyous smile
Every cold tear now feels different
As you begin to dream eyes open

Full Charge

Energy saver mode
Battery is wearing down
The charger has been lost for days
Shut off sequence commenced
"This is it…. Back-up to the cloud"

Data transfer incomplete
It can only be saved one way
It must be started up again

A friend finds a charger
It just happens to fit
In an instant, there was light
Continue transfer?
"No, it's worth keeping"
"In fact, I think it can get to full charge"

Scars

You will have these scars
And they will challenge you
But they are like the medals of a decorated soldier
Pointing towards the courage you show
Explaining your stories to be told
Counting the days you have won

Evolve

The caterpillar forms its cocoon
Just a baby to the world
Not even 3 weeks old
Yet it needs to change

A butterfly rises like a balloon
Into surrounding dangers it is hurled
But it has broken the mold
Flying across the open range

It's beaten the odds and made it to June
Riding the wind, the creature whirled
An example of one that refused to fold
As it proclaims its life exchange

Leaving the Dark

You've made the dark your home
Its light complement never shone
So like a bat you circle the night
Calling out what's lost to your sight
The kind of light that lies within
Playing your heart strings like a violin

You crave that sense of belonging
The feeling for which you've been longing
And you realize you can't find it alone
For the others help you make the light your own
With it your heart faces its next test
Finding what relieves its tension the best

Peace (A new beginning)

For the first time in my life I'm at peace
Even knowing lingering inside is the beast
Waiting to destroy me again
Trying to make me his friend
Cause I realize it is a part of me
Shaping me for better or worse
And I will never rid myself of it
Cause if I did, I wouldn't fit
Into the chaotic puzzle called life in which I sit

Mental Health Resources

1.   911
   - Use if there is immediate danger or proceed to the nearest emergency department

2.   Local Outpatient Mental Health Resources

3.   National Suicide Prevention Lifeline
   - Call 1-800-273-TALK (8255); En Español 1-888-628-9454 for free and confidential crisis counseling and mental health referrals. Available 24 hours a day, 7 days a week.

4.   The Crisis Text Line
   - Text "HELLO" to 741741 for speak with a crisis counselor regarding any type of crisis. Available 24 hours a day, 7 days a week.

5.   The Veterans Crisis Line
   - Call 1-800-273-TALK (8255)
   - For those that have trouble hearing, call 1-800-799-4889.

Chapter Significance

Chapter One:
Chapter one is called "On the Front Lines," describing those facing their illness head on. It can be easy to focus on chronic illnesses such as diabetes or heart disease because of the visible impact it has on the lives of those affected. However, according to the World Health Organization, "mental health affects one in four individuals" over a lifetime. This is a staggering figure, representing twenty-five percent of all people that will face the silent fight. In recognition of this are the first twenty-five poems.

Chapter Two:
Chapter two is entitled "POW," in reference to those that feel like prisoners of their mind. These "prisoners" more often than not do not seek the necessary medical attention for various reasons. A couple major reasons include the stigma associated with mental care and a lack of proper financial support for these services. In fact, the Substance Abuse and Mental Health Services Administration found that only around 7 percent of U.S. healthcare spending was allocated to mental health services. In recognition of this are the seven poems in chapter two.

Chapter Three:
Chapter three is called "Coming Home," signaling a sense of recovery and a regaining of control over your

illness. In my case, I have been blessed to have the resources and support available to be here today. However, some are not so fortunate and take their own lives. The National Institute of Mental Health states that the suicide rate is 14 per 100,000 and that suicide is the second leading cause of death among those 10-34. In recognition of all those affected by suicide are the fourteen poems in chapter three.

References

Levit, K., Richardson, J., Frankel, S., Mark, T., Yee, T., Chow, C., ... Pfuntner , A. (2014). Projections of National Expenditures for Treatment of Mental and Substance Use Disorders, 2010–2020. Retrieved from https://www.samhsa.gov/

Mental disorders affect one in four people. (2013, July 29). Retrieved from https://www.who.int/whr/2001/media_centre/press_release/en/

Suicide. (2019, April). Retrieved from https://www.nimh.nih.gov/health/statistics/suicide.shtml

www.ingramcontent.com/pod-product-compliance
Lightning Source LLC
LaVergne TN
LVHW011339080426
835513LV00006B/436